DISGUSTING & DREADFUL SCIENCE

Ear-Splitting Sounds
and other vile noises

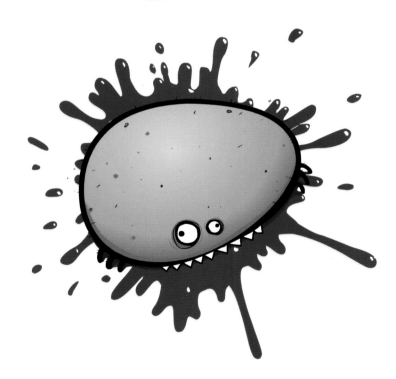

by Anna Claybourne

Crabtree Publishing Company

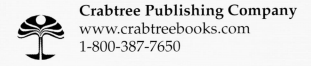

Crabtree Publishing Company
www.crabtreebooks.com
1-800-387-7650

Published in Canada
Crabtree Publishing
616 Welland Avenue
St. Catharines, ON
L2M 5V6

Published in the USA
Crabtree Publishing
PMB 59051
350 Fifth Ave, 59th Floor
New York, NY 10118

Printed in Hong Kong/092012/BK20120629

Author: Anna Claybourne
Editorial director: Kathy Middleton
Editors: Nicola Edwards, Adrianna Morganelli
Proofreader: Crystal Sikkens
Designer: Elaine Wilkinson
Picture Researcher: Clive Gifford
Production coordinator and
   Prepress technician: Amy Salter
Print coordinator: Katherine Berti

Published by Crabtree Publishing in 2013

First published in 2013 by Franklin Watts
Copyright © Franklin Watts 2013

Picture acknowledgements:
fotolia: 15b (Kirill Zdorov). Getty images: 7c (Steve Bronstein). iStockphoto.com: title page (Dean Murray), eyeball cartoon (Elaine Barker); 5t (Colleen Butler); 6bl (Jon Shulte); 8bl (ericsphotography); 9br (Jane White); 10t (Steve Skinner); 14tr & 27b (Don Bayley); 16b (hose_bw); 17t (Craig Dingle); 21tl (Manuel Velasco); 22bl (Ralf Hettler). **Jeremy Davey, Mach 1.02 Ltd**: 11t. **NASA**: 5r; 28tr (Paul Alers). **Science Photo Library**: 9cl (Bo Veisland); 13br (Thierry Berrod, Mona Lisa Production); 21bl (CNRI); 27tr (Pasieka); 29tr (AJ Photo). **Shutterstock.com**: angry monster cartoon (Yayayoyo); 4t (Verin); 4bl (Tomasz Trojanowski); 4br (photomak); 6br (3d-kot); 7t (doomu); 7br (hunta); 7bl (Jan Hyrman); 8t (Diego Cervo); 8br, 9tr, 12b & 16cl (Eric Isselée); 9cr (Roblan); 11b (Nicoleta Raftu); 12t (OZMedia); 13tr (Ivan Kuzmin); 13tl (Melinda Fawver); 14tl (blambca); 14b (Maridav); 15tr (botazsolti); 16cr (Rich Lindie); 17b (Olga Ekaterincheva); 18b (Charlene Bayerle); 19t (Luna Vandoome); 19b (Soyka); 20t (Bashutskyy); 21tr (Dudarev Mikhail); 22tr (Everett Collection); 23tl (James Steidl); 23cl (simpleman); 23b (Arthur Braunstein); 25tl (Marco Mayer); 25tr (Kitch Bain); 25cl (Dmitry Naumov); 25cr (Feng Yu); 25b (Elnur); 26tr (Clay S Turner); 26b (Tramper); 28t (David Fowler); 28b (VikaSuh); 29c (artpoint); 29br (Patrick Poendl). **Wikipedia**: 24c (Norman Bruderhofer, www.cylinder.de); 24b

All other illustrations by Graham Rich

Every attempt has been made to clear copyright. Should there be any inadvertent omission, please apply to the publisher for rectification.

**Library and Archives Canada
Cataloguing in Publication**

Claybourne, Anna
    Ear-splitting sounds and other vile noises / Anna Claybourne.

(Disgusting and dreadful science)
Includes index.
Issued also in electronic format.
ISBN 978-0-7787-0925-1 (bound).--ISBN 978-0-7787-0951-0 (pbk.)

    1. Sound--Juvenile literature. I. Title. II. Series: Disgusting and dreadful science

QC225.5.C53 2013   j534   C2012-907285-0

**Library of Congress
Cataloging-in-Publication Data**

CIP available at Library of Congress

Contents

Bang!   4

Pounded by sound   6

Weird ears   8

Boom!   10

Amazing ultrasound   12

Sounds revolting   14

Grunts, growls, squeaks, and shrieks   16

Ear-splitting science   18

Disgusting instruments   20

Incredible inventions   22

Playback!   24

Sounds nasty!   26

Sounds of the future   28

Glossary   30

Websites and Places to visit   31

Index   32

Bang!

Aaarrgh! What was that noise? You've probably heard plenty of loud, sudden sounds that made you leap out of your skin, such as fireworks, police sirens, or a big dog barking at you. Sounds are around you all the time—traffic, talking, music, machines, wind, rain, and even your own breathing. Barely a moment goes by when you can't hear one thing or another!

What is sound?

Sound is a form of **energy**, and it's actually all about movement. It happens when objects **vibrate** quickly to and fro. Usually the vibrations are so small that you can't see them, but they spread out into the air, where your ears can sense them.

Ouch!

The strongest vibrations make the loudest sounds. Some, like a rocket launch (above), a trumpet blast (below), or an explosion, are so loud they can even be painful to those people nearby.

There are a lot of reasons why objects vibrate. It can happen when two things bang or scrape against each other, or when air blows past something. Liquid flowing, an engine running, or a trumpet blasting also make sound vibrations. But why are there so many different sounds? Each sound has its own special patterns of vibrations. Combinations of different patterns, speeds, and strengths make all the varied sounds we can hear.

4

PARRRP!!!

Think of a whoopee cushion. You fill it up with air, then hope your granny will sit on it. When she does, what happens?

1. The cushion gets squashed

2. The air inside is pushed out here

3. The rushing air makes the rubber flap vibrate

4. The vibrations make a loud farting sound!

It's true...

In space, no one can hear you scream. We can only hear sound when it travels through air, or another substance, to our ears. In the **vacuum** of empty space, there's nothing for sound to move through, so nothing makes a noise.

 ## See for Yourself

Seeing sounds

Try making a few different sounds. Tap a spoon on a saucepan, clap your hands or snap your fingers, wrap elastic bands around a tissue box (right) and strum them. Different materials make different sounds, and some vibrate for longer than others. Can you see any vibrating?

Pounded by sound

Have you ever felt as if loud, rhythmic music was actually "thumping" your body? That's because it was! Sound really does hit you. In fact, you're constantly being bashed and banged by sound vibrations. Here's how it works...

Spreading sounds

The air is made up of tiny **molecules** that are too small to see. When an object, such as a whistle, vibrates, it pushes against the air molecules around it, so they start vibrating too. These air molecules push against the other molecules around them, and so on. The vibrating movement spreads out through the air as all the molecules get pushed, and start jiggling to and fro. If you are in the way, the jiggling molecules will crash into you. If they hit your ears, you will hear the sound.

Each vibration sets off a new wave of vibrations in the air, known as a sound wave.

BOOM, BOOM, BOOM

Feel the noise

Blow up and tie a balloon. Hold it up against a radio or hi-fi speaker **that's switched on. You should be able to feel the sound vibrations coming from the speaker, through the balloon, and into your fingers.**

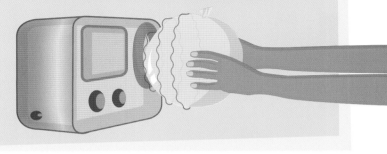

Big waves

The stronger the vibrations, the harder they push at the air molecules, and the harder they hit our ears. In other words, the stronger the vibrations, the louder the sound. The strength of a sound wave is called its **amplitude**. An alarm clock, for example, is designed to create high-amplitude sound waves to wake you up.

Smash!

Loud singing really can smash a glass. Each object has a particular speed that it vibrates at. If loud sound vibrations hit any object at the same speed, the object will start to **resonate**, or vibrate at that speed. This can make a delicate object like a wine glass shatter into pieces.

Sperm whales can aim a powerful "beam" of sound at their prey to disable it, or even kill it!

7

Weird ears

Sound vibrations are all around us, but to hear them, we need ears. Most animals have ears—even creatures that look earless, like snakes and whales. But imagine we'd never seen ears before, and we met some aliens who had them. We'd think those squiggly flaps on the sides of their heads were seriously odd! Why are they such a weird shape?

That flappy part (above) is just the outside of your ear. It's called the **pinna**, and it works like a funnel. It collects sounds and channels them into your **ear canal** (or earhole).

At the other end of the ear canal is a tightly stretched piece of skin called the **eardrum**. As sound vibrations hit it, they make it vibrate, too. The vibrations pass through three small bones, and into a spiral-shaped, gloop-filled chamber called the **cochlea**. There, tiny hairs sense the vibrations and send the sound signals to your brain. The brain makes sense of the signals, so you can understand what you're hearing.

Pinna

Ear drum

Ear bones

Cochlea

Ear canal

"Cochlea" means snail—it's named after its spiral, snail-like shape...

...however, snails themselves don't actually have any ears!

Do snakes have ears?

Some animals only have ears inside their heads, not outside. A whale's ears are just tiny holes near its eyes. Snakes don't have earholes at all, though they have cochleas and can hear. These animals don't need a pinna, as they pick up sound vibrations through their jawbones or other body parts.

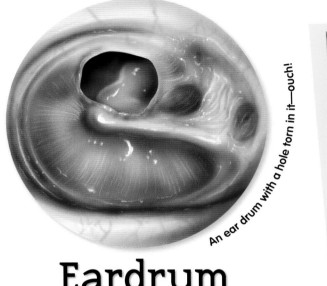

An ear drum with a hole torn in it—ouch!

Eardrum

To make it sensitive to all kinds of sounds, your eardrum is very thin and delicate. A really loud noise, like an explosion, can actually tear it open.

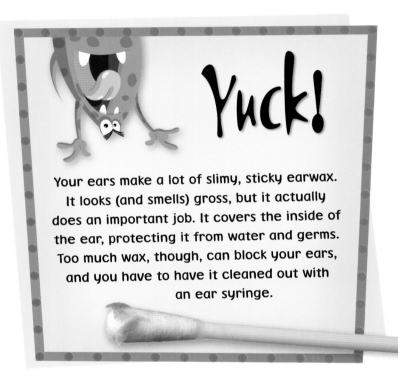

Yuck!

Your ears make a lot of slimy, sticky earwax. It looks (and smells) gross, but it actually does an important job. It covers the inside of the ear, protecting it from water and germs. Too much wax, though, can block your ears, and you have to have it cleaned out with an ear syringe.

DID YOU KNOW?

- African elephants have the biggest ears on Earth—each one is the size of a sofa!
- Whale's ears are completely blocked up with earwax.
- A long-eared jerboa's huge ears help it to cool down, as well as hear.
- Pigs have big ears and very good hearing, and seem to love music!

I'm a rock pig!

I'm into jazz.

Boom!

As a supersonic **aircraft** zooms overhead, you may hear (and feel) a massive BOOM!!! This is called a sonic boom, **and it is created when an object goes faster than the speed of sound. But how can that happen?**

How fast is sound?

The speed of sound is pretty fast. It's about 761 mph (1,225 km/h) in air. Most planes don't go that fast, but supersonic planes can. The speed of sound is different in water and other materials. Temperature can affect it, too.

Yikes!

A sonic boom doesn't usually harm people, but it can break windows and make buildings shake.

Breaking the barrier

"Breaking the sound barrier" means reaching and passing the speed of sound. But why does this make a boom? As a plane flies, it makes a noise, sending out sound waves in all directions. As it gets faster, it starts to catch up with the sound waves in front of it. When it breaks the sound barrier, it is actually going faster than the sound waves that are coming from it. They can't move away from the plane, so they all gather together into one very big, powerful **shock wave**. People on the ground hear it as an enormous BOOM as the plane passes by.

Vrooooooom!

It's not just planes that can break the sound barrier—supersonic cars have also been built. This one, Thrust SSC, was the first car to do it, reaching 763 mph (1,228 km/h) in 1997, at Black Rock Desert, U.S.A. Skydiver Felix Baumgartner broke the sound barrier with his free fall jump from the edge of space in 2012. He fell at a speed of 835 mph (1,343 km/h).

Thunder and lightning

Sound travels fast, but it's much slower than light. That's why, in a thunderstorm (below), you sometimes see a flash of lightning, then hear thunder a few seconds later. The thunder is the sound made by the lightning, but it takes longer to reach you.

See for Yourself

See it... hear it!

You can try this experiment in a school playing field or on a beach. Ask a friend to stand about 656 feet (200 meters) away from you, then make a loud noise by shouting or banging two pan lids together. You should see it happen before you hear it.

Amazing ultrasound

Ultrasound is sound that is too high-pitched for us to hear. So how do we know it's there at all—and what's it for?

Which pitch?

Pitch **means how high or low a sound is. It's decided by how fast an object (and the air around it) is vibrating. The faster it vibrates, the higher the pitch. Pitch is measured in** Hertz **(Hz), which means vibrations per second.**

EXAMPLES OF PITCH	Hz
High female singing voice	1000 Hz
Deep male singing voice	150 Hz
Middle C key on a piano	262 Hz
Whalesong	30–8000 Hz

Can't hear a thing!

Most humans can't hear sounds higher than about 20,000 Hertz, known as **ultrasound**. But some animals can. Dogs can hear up to 60,000 Hz, bats over 100,000 Hz, and porpoises as high as 160,000 Hz!

Who's calling?

Echolocation

Bats, dolphins, and some other animals use **echolocation** as a way of "seeing" objects in the dark. They send out super-high-pitched ultrasound, then listen for the echoes that bounce off objects. This lets them build up a picture of what's in front of them. It lets bats catch flying insects at night, and helps dolphins spot prey and obstacles in murky water.

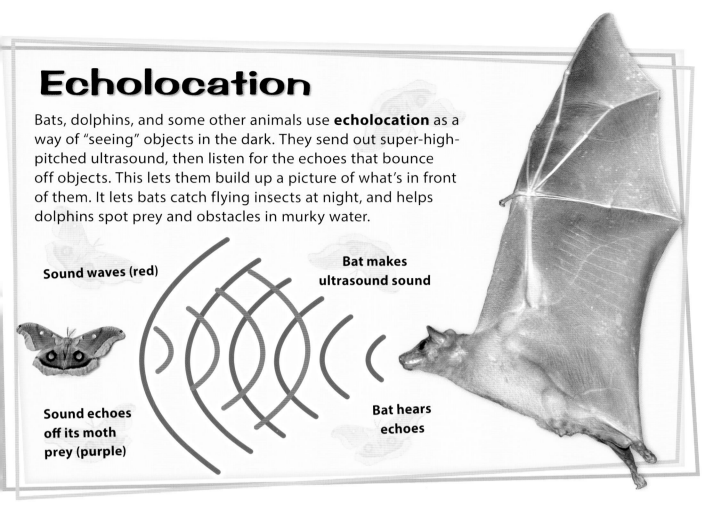

Sound waves (red)

Bat makes ultrasound sound

Sound echoes off its moth prey (purple)

Bat hears echoes

Ultra-useful!

Humans also detect and use ultrasound, with the help of high-tech machines. Ultrasound scans work like echolocation and allow us to look inside the body, at unborn babies or damaged organs.

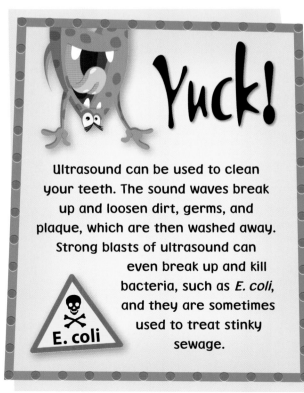

Yuck!

Ultrasound can be used to clean your teeth. The sound waves break up and loosen dirt, germs, and plaque, which are then washed away. Strong blasts of ultrasound can even break up and kill bacteria, such as *E. coli*, and they are sometimes used to treat stinky sewage.

E. coli

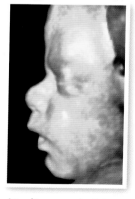

An ultrasound picture of a baby before birth.

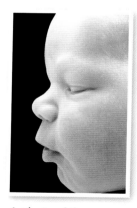

A photo of the same baby after its birth.

13

Sounds revolting

Bleuurgghh! Screeech! Drip... drip... There are some sounds that you just can't hear without flinching, feeling ill, or wanting to scream. Why is it that we find some sounds so disgusting or unbearable?

The sound of sickness

Scientists have found that the number one most disgusting sound is the sound of someone vomiting. The sounds made by going to the toilet, spitting, and coughing up phlegm are also pretty revolting. There's a good reason for this. All these things are associated with germs that could make us ill. Finding them disgusting is useful—it means we try to avoid them, and this helps us to stay healthier.

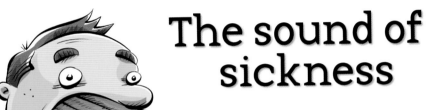

SCREECH!

Make it stop!

However, there are also a lot of other sounds that people hate that have nothing to do with germs. Scientists aren't sure why so many people can't bear the noise of squeaky polystyrene, or the scraping of a fork on a plate, a chair on the floor, or chalk on a blackboard.

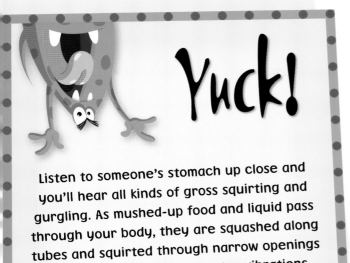

Yuck!

Listen to someone's stomach up close and you'll hear all kinds of gross squirting and gurgling. As mushed-up food and liquid pass through your body, they are squashed along tubes and squirted through narrow openings called sphincters. This creates vibrations inside your abdomen!

Now, this won't hurt a bit!

Stressful sounds

Some sounds work by making us upset. A crying baby is very stressful, and a bloodcurdling scream is terrifying. These are signals that another human being is suffering or needs help, and we should do something—or we could be in danger ourselves. Any sound that reminds us of pain is stressful too, such as a dentist's drill (above), a buzzing wasp, or a snake's hiss.

BUZZZZ

WAAAHHH!

 ## See for Yourself

Gross sound survey

Record yourself making farting, burping, spitting, coughing, and vomiting noises. (For vomit, make retching sounds while pouring water and ice cubes into the toilet). Test your friends or family to see which sounds each person finds most disgusting. Which is the winner?

Grunts, growls, squeaks, and shrieks

If you went for a walk in the rainforest, you might not see many animals, but you'd hear them chattering, buzzing, squawking, snuffling, and growling. Why do they do this?

Listen to this!

Animals use sounds to send each other all kinds of signals:

• **Get away from me!** A rattlesnake rattles its tail to warn predators off.

• **Look out! A snake!** Vervet monkeys use separate calls to warn each other when they spot a dangerous eagle, snake, or leopard.

• **I'm here, Mom!** Penguin chicks have their own unique calls, which their parents use to find them.

• **Over here!** Wolves yap and howl to each other to stay in contact when they hunt in a pack.

I want a mate!

Male and female animals make mating calls to find each other. Some frogs have a stretchy sac that they blow up like bubblegum (left) to make their mating calls. They can make grunting, chirping, croaking, barking, or clucking noises, or even electronic-sounding bleeps. Large insects called cicadas vibrate the sides of their bodies to make a grinding noise that can be as loud as a jackhammer.

Natural mimic

The amazing lyrebird from Australia can imitate any sound it hears, including cameras, chainsaws, car engines, and humans talking.

Click, whirr

Brrmmm!

Hello!

Ouch!

Tiny pistol shrimps are among the loudest of all animals. The shrimp snaps its claw to shoot out a high-pressure bubble, making a cracking sound as loud as a rocket taking off. It can stun or even kill small fish, the shrimp's prey.

Mystery of the Bloop

The "Bloop" was a very loud, low underwater sound, recorded in the Pacific Ocean in 1997. No one knows what made it, but some scientists think it could be a huge deep-sea animal that has not yet been discovered.

The chattiest animal

Of course, humans make noises too. We've developed the most complex language of any animal. Besides words, making sounds like "**tut!**" "**sigh!**" and "**ha ha ha!**" help us communicate. A few people can make really unusual sounds, like throat singers who can create two different notes at once.

Ear-splitting science

Crash! ROAR! BZZZZZZZ!!! Ouch! That was loud, but how loud? Scientists have a measuring system to show how loud and powerful sounds are. The units they use are called decibels (dB).

The decibel scale

The **decibel** scale is based on what humans can hear. It starts at zero, for a sound that's as close to silence as possible. It has no upper limit, but the loudest sounds ever heard measure around 180-200 dB.

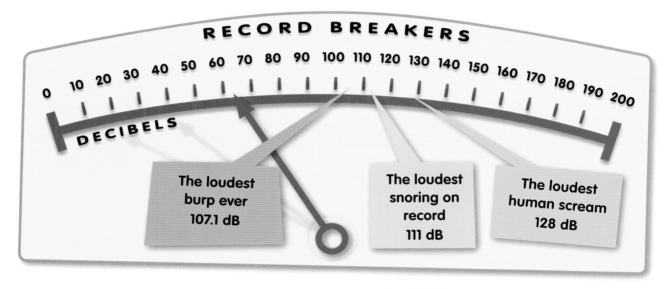

RECORD BREAKERS

0 10 20 30 40 50 60 70 80 90 100 110 120 130 140 150 160 170 180 190 200

DECIBELS

The loudest burp ever
107.1 dB

The loudest snoring on record
111 dB

The loudest human scream
128 dB

Ouch!

Sounds louder than about 120 dB are painful, and can damage your ears.

Gentle snoring
50 dB

Scale of sounds

Here you can see where a selection of disgusting and dreadful sounds register on the decibel scale, if heard close-up. The scale works in quite a weird way—20 decibels is not twice as loud as 10 decibels. Instead, it's 10 times louder and 30 decibels is 10 times louder than 20 decibels, and so on.

Rock concert 115 dB

ZZZZZZZZZ

NOISE SCALE	DECIBELS
A massive volcanic eruption	270 dB
An atom bomb exploding	250 dB
A bloodcurdling scream	120 dB
Loud rock concert	115 dB
A dentist's drill	100 dB
A cockroach hissing	90 dB
Your classroom (on a bad day)	70 dB
A loud burp	60 dB
Gentle snoring	50 dB
A deserted graveyard at night	30 dB
Very quiet breathing	10 dB

Hissing cockroach 90 dB

See for Yourself

Make it loud!

Roll a large piece of paper into a cone shape, like this.

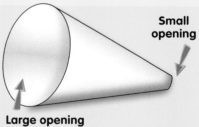

Small opening

Large opening

When you speak into the cone, do you sound louder to other people? Many musical instruments and old-fashioned record players have cones or horns where the sound comes out. They do not actually make the sound louder. Instead, they gather the sound and make it blast out in one direction, so it seems louder and travels further.

Disgusting instruments

Humans have been playing musical instruments for thousands and thousands of years. They may make a lovely sound, but they're not always made of lovely stuff!

Making a noise

Some parts of a musical instrument must vibrate to make a sound. To play different notes, a musician usually makes some part of the instrument shorter or longer, which makes faster or slower vibrations. For example, covering the holes in a recorder makes the tube longer, changing the pitch. A guitar player presses on the strings to change their length, then plucks them to make them vibrate. A shorter string vibrates faster, and makes a higher-pitched note. A longer string vibrates more slowly, and makes a lower-pitched note.

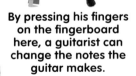

By pressing his fingers on the fingerboard here, a guitarist can change the notes the guitar makes.

Some instruments, like cymbals and most drums, only make one note.

Yuck!

People in Guyana used to make flutes out of the bones of their enemies, then dance to the music.

Bags, tubes, and stringy parts

I have a gut feeling I don't like music...

Long ago, people often made instruments from animal parts. A 40,000-year-old flute made from a vulture's bone is one of the oldest instruments ever discovered. Animal bladders or stomachs were used to make the squeezy bag in a set of bagpipes. And the strings for instruments like violins and guitars are still sometimes made of catgut. This doesn't actually come from cats. It's made from the intestines, or guts, of goats, sheep, or sometimes horses.

Your own instrument

When you speak or sing, you are vibrating stretchy muscles in your throat called **vocal chords**, by blowing air through them. You change their length to change the pitch of your voice. Here's what they look like!

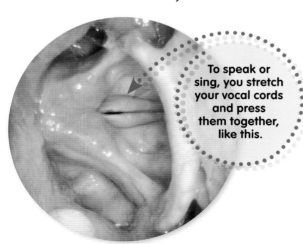

To speak or sing, you stretch your vocal cords and press them together, like this.

See for Yourself

Change the pitch

Hold a wooden or plastic ruler firmly over the edge of a table, like this. Hit the end to make it vibrate. Then move the ruler forward or backward to make the vibrating section longer and shorter. Can you hear the pitch changing? Maybe you can even play a tune.

Twang!

Incredible inventions

..._. . ._.._._`

HELP?

A telegraph operator sent and received Morse Code signals.

Hundreds of years ago, the only people you could have a chat with were the people around you. Today, you can listen to a radio presenter talking to you from hundreds of miles away. You can talk to someone on the other side of the planet, or even in space—and they can hear you!

Can you hear me?

Here are some brilliant inventions that paved the way for the world of long-distance sound technology we're used to today.

The telegraph

This invention, in the 1830s, allowed a message to be sent along an electrical wire in the form of a code, such as Morse Code. For each letter of the alphabet, the electricity was switched on and off in a pattern, making a series of clicking noises. Operators like this one would translate the signals into words and words into signals.

The telephone

"Mr. Watson, come here. I want to see you!"

This was the first phone call Alexander Bell made to his assistant in another room.

By the 1870s, several scientists, including Alexander Graham Bell, had worked out how to send the actual sound of a voice along telegraph wires. Their new invention, the telephone, used the voice's sound vibrations to make a thin sheet or "diaphragm" vibrate. It then turned these vibrations into electrical signals that could travel along a wire. At the other end, another telephone turned them back into sound vibrations.

Radio

Radio waves are a type of electromagnetic energy, similar to light. They're invisible to us, but they travel through the air in the form of waves, like this...

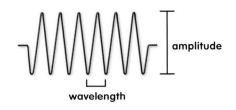

amplitude

wavelength

In the 1890s, scientists worked out how to make radio waves carry signals by changing their shape (below). The pattern in the signals could be converted into electrical signals, and played out of a speaker.

We now use radio waves to send sound long distances through the air. They work through empty space too, so we can use them to stay in touch with astronauts.

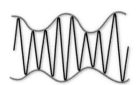

carrying radio wave signals

Story sounds

When you watch a film or TV show, or listen to a radio play, a lot of the sounds you hear, like a slap, footsteps, or someone being sick, aren't real. They are made by **foley artists** to go with the story. They do things like tread in trays of gravel, splat jelly on the floor, or smash fruit and vegetables to get the right sounds.

CLIP CLOP!

See for Yourself

Become a foley artist

Try making your own foley sounds and recording them on a computer or phone. Get your family or friends to guess what they are.

THE ART OF FOLEY

A light punch...	*punch a cabbage*
A big punch in the stomach...	*punch a piece of meat*
Breaking bones...	*snap spaghetti or celery*
Horses' hooves...	*bang coconut shells together*
Footsteps in snow...	*press cornflour in a tray*
Squealing tires...	*rub a rubber hot water bottle on a wet floor*
Skull cracking...	*smash a watermelon*

Playback!

I magine life without sound recording... no listening to your favorite songs on your headphones, no sound on films or TV shows, and no leaving a phone message. We take it for granted, but it must have been amazing when a sound was recorded for the first time.

The voice machine

The first machine that could record sound, then play it back was the **phonograph**, invented by Thomas Edison in 1877.

"Mary had a little lamb..."
This was the first thing Edison said to test out his phonograph.

4

1

2

3

1. Edison spoke into here.

2. His voice made a needle vibrate in a pattern.

3. It scratched the pattern onto a rotating cylinder, in the form of a groove.

4. When he ran the needle through the groove, the needle vibrated in the same way, and the sound of his voice came out here!

Edison hadn't expected the phonograph to work.

"I was never so taken aback in my life!"

Yuck!

For many years, disk records were made from **shellac**. It's a yellow, shiny substance made by a type of insect called the lac bug. It secretes the lac from its bottom and lays its eggs inside. Shellac is sometimes used in the coatings of some sweets!

Records were once made of shellac, but these are made of vinyl.

Modern methods

Since then, we've invented more and more ways to record sound. Early records were made on wax cylinders, then flat, round disks. Later, sound was recorded as patterns of magnetic particles on reels of tape. They were replaced by CDs read by lasers, and now sound is recorded directly into a computer's memory. Most computers have a **microphone**, which turns sound vibrations into electrical signals.

Seven-inch reels of magnetic tape were replaced by compact cassettes...

...but the tape could get tangled and break.

Amps and speakers

When we play back sound, we use other inventions to make it louder. An **amplifier** adds energy to electrical sound signals to make them stronger. A speaker turns the signals into vibrations that make the sound. These things are used without sound recording, too, at live concerts and events.

Sounds nasty!

Sounds can be useful, beautiful, musical, or soothing. But they can also be unpleasant, painful, and even deadly dangerous!

I'm off!

Killer sounds

Very loud **infrasound** (too low to hear) and ultrasound (too high to hear) can both be deadly. They can vibrate internal organs so much that they stop working, or heat up the body dangerously.

Buzz off!

Horrible sounds can be used to scare away animals. A mole-repelling machine makes sounds that rumble through the ground to scare moles, so they go elsewhere. A similar device sends sounds that bother sharks through the water to keep them away.

What's that?

Sound weapons

Very low-pitched, rumbling infrasound can be used as a weapon. Infrasound is too low to hear, but it can affect the body, damaging organs and making people feel unwell, paralyzed, scared, or dizzy. Other sonic (sound) weapons direct a very loud, shrieking noise at enemies in a narrow beam. It can stun and disable its victims and damage their hearing. It has been used to scare pirates away and stop them from attacking ships. Horrible sounds or loud, fast music have also been used as a form of torture.

Sound weapons can give your brain such a shock that it leaves you confused and helpless for short periods of time.

Yuck!

Infrasound can make people suddenly get uncontrollable diarrhea!

DID YOU KNOW?

In the Bible, the walls of Jericho are crumbled by the sound of shofars (sheep horn trumpets)—and we now know that super-powerful sound really can damage objects and buildings.

Teen repellent

There are even sound repellents for teenagers! One, called the mosquito, makes a super-annoying, high-pitched, buzzing sound that only younger people can hear, as their ears are more sensitive than adults. It's used to stop teenagers from gathering in public places. **Nice!**

AAGGGHHH!

27

Sounds of the future

W e've already invented all kinds of cool sound technology, but more is on the way! Up until now, it's only been in sci-fi movies that spaceship captains could talk to onboard computers, and people could control cars using speech. But reality is catching up with fiction and these things are appearing in real life.

How can I help?

Talking tech

Computers can synthesize, or put together, speech to enable people who can't speak to communicate with others. At the moment, they usually have to spell out what they want to say in some way. But scientists are developing mind-controlled devices that can sense brain activity. Eventually, people like eminent scientist Stephen Hawking (above) could be able to speak through a machine, just by thinking about what he or she wants to say.

Clever gadgets

Clever software can now hear what you say and translate it into instructions. Some smartphones have a computerized "assistant" inside. You can give it instructions, and it will speak back to you. Eventually, we may be able to control all our gadgets, surroundings, and even real robot servants, using just our voices.

28

Ear implants

Scientists have developed a cochlea implant, or "bionic ear," which is like an electronic ear installed inside a person's head. It is linked to the brain and turns sounds into signals that the person can understand. It is helping profoundly deaf people who want to hear.

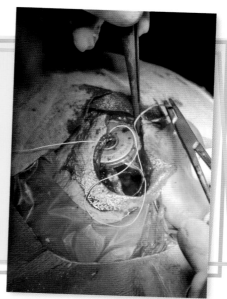

Here surgeons have opened the patient's skull to insert the device.

Yuck!

Don't forget to wipe and wash!

A Japanese company has developed a talking toilet that opens and closes its lid as it speaks to you! At the moment it's just for fun, but maybe we'll all be chatting to our toilets in the future!

My car's too quiet!

In the future, battery-powered electric cars (right) will become much more common. But there's one problem—they make hardly any noise! This could be dangerous, as we rely on car noise to tell us when a car is coming. So car companies are creating new, space-age-sounding engine noises to play through speakers when the cars are driving around busy areas.

Glossary

amplifier A machine that makes an electrical signal stronger, used to make sound louder

amplitude A measurement of the size of a sound wave or other wave

cochlea A snail-shaped part found inside the ear

decibel A unit used to measure sound intensity or loudness

ear canal A channel leading from outside the body to the inside of the ear

eardrum A thin, tightly stretched oval of skin inside the ear that picks up vibrations

echolocation A method of sensing surroundings by bouncing sounds off them

energy Power that makes things move, work, or happen

foley artist Someone who creates realistic sounds for films, TV, and radio shows

Hertz A measurement of vibrations per second, which decides the pitch of a sound

infrasound Sound too low for humans to hear

microphone A device for collecting sounds and turning them into electrical signals

molecules Tiny units that make up air and other substances

phonograph The earliest type of sound recording machine

pinna The visible part of the ear

pitch How high or low a sound is

resonate To vibrate at a particular speed

shellac A natural substance made by insects and used to make sound recording disks

shock wave A sudden, fast wave of high pressure spreading out through the air or other substances

sonic boom A loud boom made when something travels faster than the speed of sound

speaker A device that turns electrical signals into sounds

supersonic Faster than the speed of sound

ultrasound Sound too high for humans to hear

vacuum An empty space with nothing at all in it, not even air

vibrate To shake to and fro in a repeated pattern

vocal chords Bands of muscle in the human throat that vibrate to make speaking and singing sounds

Websites & Places to visit

Space Science Institute
Alien Earths: Is there anyone out there?
www.alienearths.org/online/
interactives/seti_sounds/index.php
Listen to some strange sounds—do they come from space, or our own machines?

Zoom Science: Sound
http://pbskids.org/zoom/activities/
sci/#sound
A selection of music-making activities and sound experiments.

Neuroscience for Kids: Hearing Experiments
http://faculty.washington.edu/chudler/
chhearing.html
Test your own and friends' hearing with these fascinating activities.

The Sound Site
www.smm.org/sound/nocss/top.html
A collaboration between the Science Museum of Minnesota and the Minnesota Orchestral Association exploring different aspects of sound, with activities.

The Soundry
www.library.thinkquest.org/19537
A sound site built by students for students.

Glasgow Science Centre
50 Pacific Quay
Glasgow G51 1EA, UK
www.gsc.org.uk

Magna Science Adventure Centre
Sheffield Road, Templeborough,
Rotherham S60 1DX
www.visitmagna.co.uk

Canada Science and Technology Museum
1867 St. Laurent Blvd
Ottawa, Ontario K1G 5A3
Canada
www.sciencetech.technomuses.ca/

Exploratorium
3601 Lyon Street
San Francisco, CA 94123
U.S.A.
www.exploratorium.edu/

Museum of Science
1 Science Park
Boston, MA 02114
U.S.A.
www.mos.org/

Ontario Science Centre
770 Don Mills Road
Toronto, Ontario,
Canada
www.ontariosciencecentre.ca

Index

air 4, 5, 10, 12, 21, 23
air molecules 6, 7
aircraft 10
amplifier 25
amplitude 7, 23
animals 8, 9, 12, 13,
    16–17, 19, 21, 26
baby 13, 15
bats 12, 13
Bell, Alexander Graham 22
Bloop 17
brain 8, 27, 28, 29
cars 11, 17, 28, 29
cicadas 16
cochlea 8, 9
cochlea implants 29
decibels 18–19
dogs 12
dolphins 13
eardrum 8, 9
ears 4, 6, 7, 8–9, 18, 27, 29
earwax 9
echolocation 13
Edison, Thomas 24
experiments
    Become a foley artist 23
    Change the pitch 21
    Feel the noise 7
    Gross sound survey 15
    Make it loud! 19
    See it... hear it! 11
    Seeing sounds 5

foley artists 23
frogs 16
Hawking, Stephen 28
Hertz 12
hissing cockroach 19
human communication
    4, 17, 22, 28
infrasound 26, 27
inventions 22, 25
lightning 11
lyrebird 17
mating calls 16
microphone 25
Morse Code 22
music 4, 6, 9, 20–21, 27
musical instruments
    4, 19, 20–21, 27
noises
    body 5, 15
    disgusting 14–15
    loud 4, 9, 11, 18–19, 27
    painful 15, 18
    stressful 15
phonograph 24
pigs 9
pinna 8, 9
pistol shrimps 17
pitch 12, 13, 20, 21, 27
porpoises 12
radio 7, 22, 23
recording (sound)
    15, 17, 23, 24–25

records (disks) 25
resonate 7
robots 28
sharks 26
shellac 25
shock wave 10
singing 7, 12, 17, 21
skydivers 11
snails 8
snakes 8, 9, 15, 16
sonic boom 10
sound barrier 10, 11
sound recording (see recording)
sound repellents 26, 27
space 5, 11, 22, 23
speaker 7, 23, 25, 29
speed of sound 4, 7, 10–11
supersonic 10–11
tape 25
telegraph 22
telephone 22, 23, 24, 28
Thrust SSC 11
thunder 11
toilets 14, 15, 29
ultrasound 12–13, 26
vibrations 4–5, 6, 7, 8,
    9, 12, 15, 20, 22, 25
vocal chords 21
vomiting 14, 15
weapons (sonic) 27
whales 7, 9, 12
whoopee cushion 5